MW00891695

# Evie Rose is a Talented Girl!

# EVIE ROSE

# IS A

# TALENTED

# GIRL!

By

**Robert E. Burtt &**

**Geri A. Paquette**

# Burtt, Robert E.
# &
# Grace A. Paquette

## *Evie Rose is a Talented Girl!*

Copyright 2024 by Robert E. Burtt
All rights reserved. No part of this book may be reproduced
or transmitted in any form without the written permission of
the authors.

ISBN-10: 9798342470773

Manufactured in the United States of America

# Talented Girl Publishing

By

Createspace, an Amazon Company
172 Trade Street
Lexington, KY 40511

1st Edition

Merry Christmas 2024

From

Papa & Gigi!

Evie Rose
is a Talented Girl!
She can do so
many things and
is always ready to
try new projects!
Just look at this
Water color painting
She did for Mama!

Even just "hanging
around" the house,
Evie is always
Drawing, painting,
and trying out new
Ways to make "Art."
She loves to draw,
Paint, and color!
She is sooo talented!

Evie had a great
Time designing,
And building,
A gingerbread house
during last year's
Christmas Holiday
Season! It looked
Very artistic, and...
Tasted even Better!!!

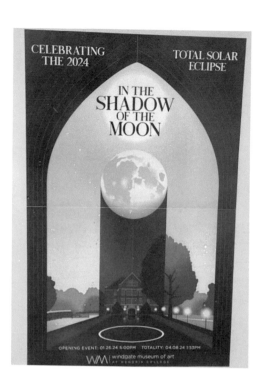

In 2024, Arkansas
Was in the path of a
Solar Eclipse! It was
a Big Deal!
The Windgate Museum
Of Art at Hendrix College
called for all school kids
To paint pictures with
An "Eclipse Theme."
Evie was one of
The Winners!

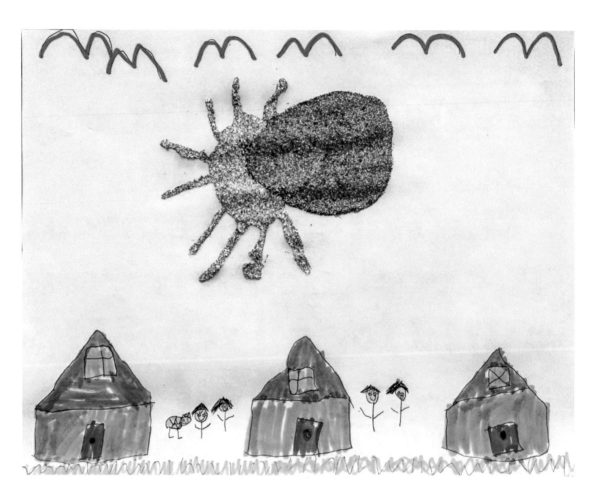

Majestic Eclipse over Maumelle by Evie Rose Burleson

# Mama was
# Soooo Proud of Evie!

Evie Rose went to
A Cat Show!
She simply
LOVES
Kittys!!!

Evie goes
To Kindergarten
At Maumelle
Charter Elementary
School!
They're called
The Falcons!
She likes her
school a lot!

Evie having
A good "hair day."
Even girls
That are
Talented need
To look Nice!
She is such a
Happy Girl!

**Last Christmas,
Evie played
an Angel
in the
Holiday Pageant
At CDC!
She is always
As cute as
an Angel. She's
as Nice as one Too!**

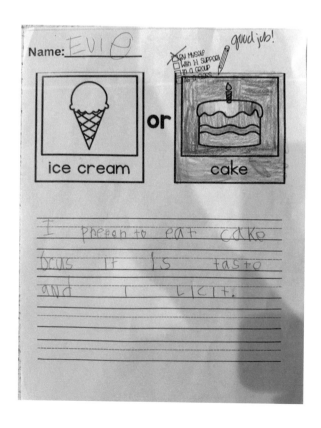

Name: Evie

good job!

ice cream **or** cake

I prefer to eat cake
breus it is tasto
and I likit.

Evie
Goes to school
Each morning! She
Loves Kindergarten.

Here's a
Sample of one
Of her
Assignments.
She is sooo Smart!

Even Talented
Girls need good Friends.

Adalyn is
One of Evie's
"Besties!"

They love playing
Together at
School and
"Hanging Out."

**Evie Rose Graduated
from Kindergarten
at Maumelle
Charter Elementary!
In just a few years—
High School!**

KINDERGARTEN

## CERTIFICATE

is presented to

## EVIE ROSE BURLESON

for successfully completing Kindergarten

on this 16th day of May 2024

at Maumelle Charter Elementary School

*Mrs. Brittany Holland*
**TEACHER**

*Maumelle Charter Elementary*
*Welcomes you to*

# KINDERGARTEN
# GRADUATION

*May 16, 2024*

*Processional*

*Musical Performance*
On My Way
It's My Time To Shine

*Introduction*

*Presentation of Certificates*

Parents,
During the ceremony we ask that you stay off of the carpeted area and that you stay for the entire graduation. We ask that you exit quickly so that the gym and parking lot can be prepared for the award assembly for older grades.

**Mrs. Barker**
Elleny Acosta
Lucas Apple
Yadah Bailey
Laiyah Becker
Micaiah Bonney-Donkor
Bristol Bronson
Ayden Cox
Logan Crouch
Naomi Freeman
Kade Holloman
Benjamin Hornbeck
Emmy LaCour
Ty Miller Jr.
Kendall Neal
Joshua Norris
Stephen Pruss
Jack Sparrow
Archer Spradlin
Ellie West
Jasper Zhang

**Mrs. Leigh**
Kori Bell
Charlie Caviness
Evvie Conley
Zeke Cowdery
Londyn Davis
Riley Davis
Jacob Dipasquale
Charlene Douthit
Ethan Cruz Gabriel Gomez
Ava Jackson
Emilia Lewis
Olivia Maier
Milan Marleneanu
Emmanuel Olson
Jack Rowe
Hunter Schnell
Caleb Simmons
Leah Slagle
Brody Wilson

**Mrs. Holland**
Adalyn Bearden
Norah Blake
Ali Bland
Everly Burleson
Tristan Chapel
Ruth Dunavant
Bella Duzan
Gabriel Green Jr.
Logan Hankins
Khari Holden
Olivia Jenkins
Brooke-Anne Keesee
Silas Kemper
Scarlett Leatherwood
Redd Macon
Holden Mellenthin
Raiden Nelson
Hinslei Propps
Brewer Simpson
Rhett Uting

**Mrs. Sites**
Indie Behnke
James Carroll
Pepper Doroski
Dymeatrius Edwards
Ashlyn Erby
Dustin Le
Barrett Lowery
Ridley Matthey
Kellie Meeks
Phoenix Moon
Eliam Ochterbeck
Amarachi Okoli
Royce Perry
Blair Smith
Kalayah Strachan
Hank Terry
Hudson Tolliver
Matthew Watson
Lyla White
Saylor Young

# It was a Great day! Mama, Dada, and Papa-Gigi were so Proud!

Talented Girls
Like Evie
Usually
Win
Awards!
She
Had so
Much fun at
Graduation!

Evie
Went to a
Roller skating Party!
For her first time,
She was pretty good!
Of course, Talented
Girls can learn
Just about
Anything!!

**Summertime!
That means
The Pulaski County
Fair! Talented
Girls need a break
and a chance to
Enjoy Trying some
Rides!
It was hot, but Evie
Had a lot of FUN!**

Of course, it
Wouldn't be fun
for Evie unless
Knox came along!
He's a great little
Brother and they
Have such a great
Time together!

Evie is very
Serious about her
Art projects.
She paints or draws
Pictures almost every
single, day.
Her "work station" will,
One day, become a
Studio!

A little makeup,
Some lipstick,
a Kitty t-shirt,
and our talented
girl is ready to face
the day. Looking
GOOD Evie!

**Talented Girls
Also like to have fun.
Evie, Knox,
And Roxie
Laughing and
"chilling" on the
Couch at home.
Good times!**

Evie enjoys
"Splash Pads" like
This one in Sherwood.
Lots of slides, sprays,
Water, and FUN!!!

Usually when,
Evie comes home
From school, she gets
A snack, unwinds
A little, and then
Gets started on an
Art project. She
Is very serious,
and Very Talented!

Have we mentioned
That Evie LOVES
Kitties? They
Are her
Favorite!

First day of
FIRST GRADE!
Evie is now
A "BIG KID!"
At
Maumelle Charter
Elementary School!
It's a great place
For a Talented Girl!

2023 (K)

2024 (1st)

Not sure how Evie
Grew so fast, but
There is no stopping
Her now!
What a big girl!
What a talented Girl!

Mama just
Had to take
A few extra pictures!
I mean, How often
Does a Talented
Girl start
First Grade?
Just once!
Have a great Time
Evie!!!

First Day of
Elementary School!
Oh My!
Evie had a good
First day and really
Likes her Teacher
And the other kids
In her class!

**The crown says
It all! Evie
Is off on a
New adventure
in school! Just the
Place for a very
Talented Girl!!**

Evie got
A "Star Pupil"
Award one day,
and a wristband
for being a
good example on
another day. No surprise
that such a Talented
Girl is doing well at
School!

Evie's talents
In Art are
amazing!
One day she
Painted a
"Space Robot."
She also
Decorated a bandaid
That she wore to
School! Wondeful!

On "Grandparents Day"
Evie showed Papa-Gigi
all around her
School. She helped
them paint a "special"
project, got them cookies,
and introduced her
Classmates!
Way to go Evie!

Evie and Roxie.
A talented Girl
And her dog.
Same Pose,
Different Nose!

Evie's little
Brother Knox
Is 5 years Old!
Evie likes his
Stylish sunglasses!
Wonderful
picture Evie!
She is talented
AND Cute!

**It's Halloween!**
**Knox was Leonardo, and**
**Evie chose a really great**
**Costume!**
**A Kitty Squishmallow!**
**Perfect!**
**Evie LOVES Kittys**
**AND she loves**
**Squishmallows!**
**Well Done Evie!!!**

# THINGS EVIE SAYS:

"Mama, I want to go to Gigi's to make some money." (Mommy) "You can do that here." --"But Mama, do you *Have* any money?"

"It's AMAZING! I LOVE it!!"

"Momma, while you're up, can you get me more milk?"

"I love Meoow! She's sooo Cute!!"

"Hi Mr. Davis!" (next-door neighbor)

"It's Aunt Joan!"

"Are you fooling me?"

"Gigi is a really good Artist!"

"Mama, my tongue is broken. It's not Attached to my Mouth!" (AT 2 A.M.)

"When am I going to lose a tooth?"

"But Gigi lets me!"

"Hey gurlfriend! Hey gurlfriend! Whass Up? Whass Up?"

"It's 'dinner,' not 'supper!'"

"Thanks Gurlfriend!"

"Papa, I already TOLD you that? Didn't you Listen?"

"That's making me NUTS!"

To be continued...

Made in the USA
Columbia, SC
07 November 2024

45354898R00044